SPORTS GREAT
KARL
MALONE

—Sports Great Books —

SPORTS GREAT
KARL
MALONE

Jeff Savage

—Sports Great Books—

ENSLOW PUBLISHERS, INC.
44 Fadem Road   P.O. Box 38
Box 699   Aldershot
Springfield, N.J. 07081 Hants GU12 6BP
U.S.A.   U.K.

Library of Congress Cataloging-in-Publication Data
Savage, Jeff, 1961-
    Sports great Karl Malone / Jeff Savage.
        p. cm. — (Sports great books)
    Includes index.
    ISBN 0-89490-599-6
    1. Malone, Karl—Juvenile literature. 2. Basketball players—United
States—Biography—Juvenile literature. [1. Malone, Karl. 2. Basketball players.
3. Afro-Americans—Biography.] I. Title. II. Series.
GV884.M18S28 1995
796.323'092—dc20
[B]
                                                                94-3709
                                                                   CIP
                                                                    AC

Printed in the United States of America

10 9 8 7 6 5 4 3 2 1

Illustration Credits: Louisiana Tech, pp. 31, 33, 35; Norm Perdue, pp. 18, 56, 58,
60; Utah Jazz, pp. 9, 11, 14, 39, 40, 42, 44, 50, 52, 54.

Cover Photo: Norm Perdue

Contents

Chapter 1

Larry Bird was at the baseline, practicing his jump shot. Charles Barkley was in the paint, working on soft hooks. Patrick Ewing stood under the basket, grabbing rebounds.

It was the day before the 1988 NBA All-Star Game, and basketball's best players were on the court in Chicago Stadium, getting loose.

At the other basket, Clyde Drexler and Alvin Robertson took turns shooting twenty footers, while Hakeem Olajuwon and Xavier McDaniel playfully tried to out-muscle one another for rebounds. Magic Johnson stood off to one side, smiling, bouncing a basketball, up and down, up and down, with his left hand. Everyone was having a good time. This was the place to be if you were a basketball star.

Camera crews and reporters were buzzing about, getting interviews from some of the players. A large group had gathered at one end of the arena, getting comments from Michael Jordan, the game's newest superstar. Kareem Abdul-Jabbar, the tall center from the Los Angeles Lakers, stood nearby, talking with another group.

Not too far away, another player stood before a cluster of newspaper writers. He was tall and muscular, and he was smiling. "This is the media capital of the world right here," the player was saying to the reporters. "And it seems like you all want to talk to me, Karl Malone. It's a fairy tale. I know it's the All-Star game. But I had no idea it would be like this."

Who was this young man named Karl Malone? The media was finding out. "They were asking everything," he said later. "About my background. My hometown. My future plans. About my attitude toward the media. Whatever you can think of, they asked it. It was awesome."

Karl Malone was in the national spotlight for the first time, and it nearly overwhelmed him.

"Everything has just happened so quickly," he told reporters, and indeed it had. A year earlier, in his second season as a pro, it was clear that Karl had become the best player on his team—the Utah Jazz. "It's not even close," Jazz coach Frank Layden had been telling everyone. "He's head and shoulders above the rest." Malone was so impressive as a power forward that the Jazz felt safe trading their only proven scorer, Adrian Dantley, to the Detroit Pistons. At the end of the season the town of Salt Lake City, where the Jazz play their home games, hosted a "Karl Malone Day" in honor of their new basketball star. The Jazz rewarded Malone with a new five-year contract for $1 million a year—a great deal at the time.

The one thing Karl didn't get was national attention. The Boston Celtics still had the attention of fans in the Northeast. The Detroit Pistons and Chicago Bulls were the heavyweights of the Midwest. The Los Angeles Lakers and Portland Trail Blazers made all the noise on the West Coast. People didn't know much about the little team nestled in the Wasatch Mountains of Utah. Karl Malone had a great season, but no

Until his first appearance in the 1988 NBA All-Star Game, few had heard of Karl Malone.

one outside Salt Lake City really noticed. Naturally, he didn't make the All-Star team that year. "I was disappointed," Karl admitted. "Yet, I knew that I had been in the league only two years and would someday get my chance."

Malone played better than ever in his third season. As the 1988 All-Star Game approached, he was among the NBA leaders in both scoring and rebounding. People couldn't help but notice him now. Still, in the final week of balloting by fans across the country, Malone was running fourth in the voting for forwards for the Western Conference team. It wasn't until the last few days that he shot up to second place to earn a starting role. At twenty-four years of age, he and Chicago Bulls guard Michael Jordan were the youngest starters in the game.

Karl stood before the group of reporters and explained how he felt. "This is something I've always dreamed about and hoped to do one day, and now that dream is coming true," he said. "There are thousands of guys every year who wish they could play in the NBA. Not only am I fortunate to play in the NBA, but now I'm on the All-Star team. It's too much to believe sometimes. It's an honor to be..." Malone was interrupted. Isiah Thomas was tapping him on the shoulder. "Congratulations, Strongman," the Pistons guard said as he shook Malone's hand. "And Adrian [Dantley] told me to say hello."

Karl smiled. "Thanks," he said. "Tell him hello, too."

Isiah Thomas turned and walked away. Karl looked down and shook his head in disbelief. "My reaction to all this?" he said to another question by a reporter. "Unbelievable."

"Hey, Karl," someone said from behind him. Karl turned around. It was Magic Johnson.

"You should've made it last year," Magic said, referring to the 1987 All-Star Game. Karl just smiled. He was too

In the 1988 NBA All-Star Game, Malone faced the greatest players of the Eastern Conference. Among them were Isiah Thomas, of the Detroit Pistons, and Charles Barkley, who was playing for the Philadelphia 76ers.

embarrassed to say anything. Finally, after Magic had left, Karl said softly, "I never imagined things like this could happen to me. This has been the highlight of my career so far."

Things were about to get even better.

The next day, as the crowd crammed into Chicago Stadium and the teams warmed up, Karl looked around and realized he was in the presence of some of the all-time greats. "I felt like grabbing a camera and taking pictures of all these guys," he said.

Then, while the lineups were being introduced, Karl began to get very nervous. He was sitting on the bench between Magic Johnson and Kareem Abdul-Jabbar. "What did you guys feel like before your first All-Star Game?" Karl asked them.

"I was excited and nervous," Magic said. "Don't worry, Karl. Everybody's scared their first time."

Kareem leaned over and whispered, "Just think about your friends and family back in Louisiana."

The advice worked. Karl relaxed a little.

Karl was informed by West coach Pat Riley that he would be guarding Eastern Conference starting center Moses Malone. Karl couldn't believe it. Moses had been his boyhood idol. "I never had a lot of childhood heroes, but I always idolized Moses," Karl explained.

One of Karl's strengths as a player is his intensity. He gets so fired up to beat the other team that he doesn't even shake hands with his opponents before the game. For the All-Star Game, he abandoned this ritual. As the starting lineups assembled at center court for the opening tip, Karl reached out and shook the hand of Moses Malone.

Then the ball was tossed in the air. It was tipped by Hakeem Olajuwon and the game began. On the West's first possession, Magic Johnson dribbled at the top of the key, then whipped a pass inside to Malone. Karl turned to face the basket, leaned in against Moses, avoided a swipe at the ball by Larry Bird, and let go with a five-footer. Swish! Thirty-five seconds into the game, Karl Malone had scored a basket for the West. A minute later, Magic worked the ball inside to Karl again. The six-foot-nine-inch power forward pounded the ball once to the floor as he moved to the hoop to bank a two-footer off the glass. Good! Another basket for Malone!

Karl was nicknamed "The Mailman" by a sportswriter when he played at Louisiana Tech University because he always delivered. Now he was delivering in a big way, in front of 18,000 fans in Chicago Stadium, with millions more watching on television. Two more times in the first quarter Malone scored baskets on inside power moves. He controlled the boards, too, pulling down five rebounds. After one quarter, Karl Malone was the best performer in the All-Star Game. And the West was leading, 32–27.

"I wasn't really worried about scoring points," Karl said later. "But—get this—we came out and they were running plays for *me*! I'm in my first All-Star Game and they ran the first play for *me*. I couldn't believe it was happening to me."

Among the customs of an All-Star Game is that everybody gets a chance to play. So Malone sat on the bench for most of the second quarter while other forwards played. He scored one basket late in the quarter, but by then, the East had taken a six-point lead.

Karl scored four points in the first three minutes of the third quarter, then sat down and watched Michael Jordan and Dominique Wilkins take command of the game for the East. With a quarter to go, the East lead was up to ten.

As the fourth quarter began, Alex English and James Worthy were in the game at the two forward spots for the West. Karl was beginning to wonder it he would get to play again. Then, with nine minutes left in the game, coach Pat

With rim-bending dunks, Malone earned national recognition by the end of the 1988 All-Star Game.

Riley sent Karl back in. "The Mailman" would play the rest of the way, and he would deliver eight more points.

With four minutes left, Isiah Thomas drove down the lane for the East. Hakeem Olajuwon stole the ball and tapped it forward to Magic Johnson. Magic pushed it upcourt with a couple of dribbles, then rifled a pass downcourt to Karl Malone, who was gliding toward the basket from the right side. Karl caught the ball in midair and slammed it home with an incredible dunk!

"Magic, you threw a heck of a pass," Karl told Johnson.

"No," Magic responded. "You went and got it."

The Eastern Conference won the game anyway by a score of 138–133.

The big surprise, however, was the performance of this new kid named Karl Malone. In 33 minutes of playing time, Karl had led the Western Conference in scoring with 22 points, and in rebounding with 10.

"Karl played a great game," West coach Pat Riley said. "I couldn't keep him on the floor enough. If any player on our team deserved to be Most Valuable Player, it would've been Karl Malone."

In the locker room, Karl gathered up his belongings for the plane trip back to Salt Lake City. His career would change because of this day. He would become one of the most popular players in the NBA. Certainly, more people would know about the Utah Jazz. But Karl didn't think about any of this. He only thought about what a good time he'd had.

"This weekend," he said to the media, "I've been like a kid in a candy store. And I want to thank all the people who made it possible. The Jazz front office. My teammates. It was my body here this weekend. But others made it happen for me. And if I never make it here again, at least I've got this game to look back on and remember."

Chapter 2

Karl Malone grew up in the tiny town of Summerfield, in northern Louisiana. He was born on July 24, 1963, in the nearby town of Bernice, because there was no hospital in Summerfield. His father, J. P. Malone, died of cancer in 1977, when Karl was fourteen. Karl was raised by his mother, Shirley.

Karl had eight brothers and sisters. Eddie, Marilyn, Danny, Patricia, Kenneth, Jenny, and Terry were older than Karl. Tiffany was younger.

The Malones lived in a large white house in the woods. Karl's mother came from a family of sharecroppers. Sharecroppers are farmers who live and work on a farm and pay rent to the owner of the land with a portion of the food they grow. Mrs. Malone used her knowledge of farming to grow most of her family's food.

There was a big garden alongside the house where the Malones grew corn, potatoes, beans, collard greens, and other vegetables. Behind the house were chickens in a coop and hogs in a pen for meat. Next to the coop and pen was a henhouse for eggs.

One of Karl's chores as a boy was to fetch the eggs from the henhouse. The hens sat on their nests high up on a shelf so that marauding animals couldn't get to them. Karl would stand up on a chair, reach up into the nests, and collect the eggs. This was a slippery task. One time, Karl tried to hold too many eggs at once. One of the eggs tumbled from his grasp and he tried to catch it. Suddenly he lost his balance and came crashing down as the eggs broke all over him in a gooey mess. Karl ran crying into the house.

Around the Malone house there were some terrific opportunities for mischief. Karl was playing with the chickens in the coop one day when he noticed a skinny chicken waddling around in a corner. He grabbed the chicken by the neck and carried it into the house. What a wonderful pet this pokey chicken would make. When Karl's mother came home, she found Karl sitting on the living room floor with the chicken.

"Karl, what is that chicken doing in here?" Mrs. Malone screamed.

"It's my chicken, mama," Karl said.

"Get that chicken out of this house, right now!"

"But mama, this chicken likes it in here."

"Karl, get that chicken back in the coop. Besides, it doesn't look so well."

"I know, mama. It's kinda droopy."

Karl picked up the chicken and headed outside with it. But he stopped at the door. "I got an idea, mama. Why don't we kill it and eat it?"

The chicken went back in the coop.

Karl's ace buddy was Don Gilmore, who lived across the fence. One summer day Karl and his brother, Terry, walked with Don down the street to Mr. Stevenson's watermelon patch. Mr. Stevenson wasn't home. The boys went into the

Since he was a boy, Malone's favorite sport has been basketball. He made his first dunks through his mother's arms.

watermelon patch, broke open a watermelon, and ate it. Then they ate a second watermelon. Then another. Before long, they were smashing all the watermelons in the patch. When Mr. Stevenson got home and found the mess, he had a good idea who was responsible. Karl was home when Mr. Stevenson showed up at the front door. He knew he was in big trouble now.

"I got some bad news for you, Shirley," Mr. Stevenson said to Karl's mother. "I think your boys and their buddy busted up my watermelons."

Karl confessed. His mother was furious. "I'll pay for the watermelons," she said to Mr. Stevenson.

"No, no," he said. "You work hard for your money."

"OK, then," she said. "I've got an idea how we can resolve this. First, though, Karl and Terry are in for a big whupping."

The boys had to carry several pieces of firewood down the street every day and place them on Mr. Stevenson's front porch, and then put one log in his fireplace. They did this for six months. That was after the "big whupping." Mrs. Malone used a leather belt that she got from the sawmill where she worked. She also worked in salt mills, corn fields, and cotton fields—anywhere she could earn enough money to support her children.

Karl's favorite sport was basketball. The family couldn't afford a hoop and backboard, so Karl's mother would stand with her arms in a circle in front of her, in the shape of a basket. Karl and Terry would practice shooting a rubber ball through their mother's arms. Mrs. Malone didn't always have time to be a basketball hoop. So Karl put up a hoop in the front yard by fastening both ends of a bicycle spoke to a tree.

Karl went to church with his family every Sunday. After the sermon, they would return home and gather in the living room to discuss what they had learned. Mrs. Malone would go around the room to each of her children, one by one.

"Danny, tell me something different," she would say. Danny would explain what he learned.

"Patricia, tell me something different."

"Kenneth, tell me something different."

"Jenny, tell me something different."

Around the room she would go.

One time, the preacher told a story about the beggar Lazarus. Soon after, the Malones were back at home, going around the room, explaining what had they learned about Lazarus. Eventually, Mrs. Malone got to Karl, who was eight at the time. "Karl, tell me something different," she said.

Karl sat on the floor and stared up at his mother. For a long time, he said nothing. Finally, he spoke up.

"I don't know, mama. I'm kinda confused. But I know he's been dead a long time."

There wasn't much for grown-ups to do in Summerfield. The town had just one store, the Butch Bays Grocery, and one school, Summerfield, which taught children from kindergarten through high school. If grown-ups wanted to go out for a fancy evening, they had to drive to Haynesville to the west, Ruston to the south, or Junction City to the north at the Arkansas border.

For young boys, excitement in Summerfield was another matter altogether. The town's population consisted of about 200 people and what seemed like a million squirrels, raccoons, deer, and other animals. Karl spent almost all of his time catching small animals. When he grew older, he learned to shoot a gun.

One afternoon when Karl was fourteen, he and Terry went into the woods behind the house to hunt squirrels. They brought with them a 12-gauge shotgun with light-load shells.

Deep in the woods, about a mile from home, Karl and Terry heard a noise. They looked up and there was a deer—right in front of them. Karl took aim and pulled the trigger. Boom! The deer fell over. Karl shot it again. And again. And again. He filled the deer full of squirrel shot until it was dead. Terry stayed with the deer while Karl ran home to get his mother. The family would get to eat venison for a week.

Mrs. Malone drove back with Karl in the '64 Ford truck to where Terry was waiting with the deer. Instead of putting the deer in the bed of the truck, Karl insisted that they lay the deer over the top of the cab. On the ride home, Karl shouted out the window, "We got him! We got him!"

Mrs. Malone cooked some of the venison that night, but it was so full of squirrel shot and gunpowder that they couldn't eat it.

Karl enjoyed fishing even more than hunting. After he caught his first fish as a five-year-old, he was hooked. Karl and his mother were standing on the edge of a private pond stocked with bass, each using a cane pole, when a fish bit on his line. He felt the pole jerk and held on. "Look, mama. I caught a fish!" he yelled. "I caught a fish!"

"Well, go on and pull him out," she said. "I'm busy doing my own fishing." Mrs. Malone wanted Karl to handle this fishing business on his own.

Karl romped around so much through the backwoods of Summerfield that there was barely time to study. He attended school, but doing his homework was another matter. "He would bring his books home from school on Friday afternoons and throw them in the corner," Shirley Malone says. "He wouldn't touch them again until Monday morning."

Mrs. Malone was so busy with work that she didn't have time to watch over Karl. Every year on the first day of school she would call the principal of Summerfield School, Mr.

Scriber, and remind him that she didn't have time to run down there if Karl got in trouble. "Mr. Scriber," she would say, "I give you my permission to whup Karl if he gets out of line."

One time, Karl got in trouble and had to go to the principal's office. Mr. Scriber let him choose his punishment—a whupping or a three-day suspension. For Karl, this was an easy choice. He didn't care much for school in the first place, and three days off would be fine with him. Mr. Scriber sent Karl home.

Karl informed his mother of his choice of punishment that night. She was not happy.

Karl was at school the next morning, and his mother was with him. They went directly to the principal's office.

"Mrs. Malone, what are you doing down here?" Mr. Scriber asked. "I thought you didn't have the time."

"I made an exception," she said.

"Did Karl tell you about his punishment—a three-day suspension?" the principal asked.

"Yes, he did, Mr. Scriber. And Karl has changed his mind. He has decided that he wants that whuppin' after all."

Karl looked at his mother. He had made no such decision.

"But, mama," Karl said. "I never . . ."

"And Mr. Scriber," she interrupted, still looking at the principal, "after you whup him, and send him back to class, be sure he gets home right after school, so I can whup him again."

This wasn't the worst thing Karl ever did at school. He received such a bad report card one time that he was sure he'd get punished if he showed it to his mother. So Karl tried to convince his sister Marilyn to sign it. Marilyn took the dreaded report card and disappeared into the kitchen with it. Karl thought she had gone to get a pen. A moment later, though, out came the report card in the hand of Karl's mother! Karl was sent to his room.

Like other schools, Summerfield required students to have a 2.0 grade-point average (a "C" average) to participate in after-school athletics. Karl failed to achieve a 2.0 average in his freshman year, so although he practiced each day with the team, he was never issued a uniform. During games, he had to sit in the stands. This made him feel left out. He wished he could find the time to study, but there were so many distractions in Summerfield, so many squirrels to hunt, so many fish to catch.

Chapter 3

Howard Moss, the boys' basketball coach at Summerfield, knew what kind of team he would have if he could just get Karl Malone into a uniform. He had taught Karl the basic moves in practice as a freshman. Karl knew all of the team's plays, and at six feet three inches, he was tall enough and talented enough to play forward. But his poor grades made him ineligible to play.

Coach Moss figured things would be different in Karl's sophomore year, but he was wrong. Karl continued to goof off instead of studying. The situation was getting urgent. Basketball practice would be starting in a week, and the games would begin soon after.

Report cards were due out, and Karl admitted to Coach Moss one day that his grades would surely be poor again. After that, the next grade session wouldn't end until the middle of January. By then, half the basketball season would be over. "Well, you're sure to miss quite a few games," Coach Moss said. "But if you start studying now and get better grades on your January report card, you'll be able to join the team for the second part of the season."

"I'll try," Karl said.

Karl practiced with the team. During games, though, he sat in the stands, just as he had in his freshman year. The difference this time was that he sat with his school books.

Mid-January finally arrived and grades were handed out. Coach Moss was the first to hear the good news. "I made it," Karl told him, holding out his report card. "I made the team."

Karl was immediately inserted into the starting lineup. He would play forward. The Summerfield Rebels had a losing record, but the playoffs were not yet out of reach.

The Rebels had a six-foot-seven-inch, 250-pound center named Jeff Homes, and a pure shooting guard named Sam Pitts. With Karl in the lineup, opponents could no longer double-team Jeff or Sam. Summerfield began winning. Karl averaged more than 15 points a game. The Rebels qualified for the playoffs with an 18-17 record—just barely.

Summerfield's biggest rival was nearby Pineview High. The two teams played one another eight times during the year, and Pineview had won six games. After both teams won in the first round of the Louisiana Class C playoffs, they met again. The Louisiana prep basketball playoffs are structured in such a way that if a team loses once in the regionals, it could still be alive in the playoffs. A good thing, too, because Summerfield lost to Pineview once again. Coach Moss was frustrated that he couldn't beat the rival school. He *had* to keep his team charging forward. Another loss and the Rebels' season would be over.

Charge ahead they did. Summerfield won its next four games to advance to the Louisiana state championship game. The title game would be played one hundred miles to the south, in a coliseum arena in the city of Alexandria. Summerfield's opponent? Pineview High.

It was a close game all the way. Pineview led by four

points at the half, but Summerfield tied it in the third quarter. The game seesawed back and forth the rest of the way, and at the final buzzer, it was still tied. Overtime! In the last few seconds of the extra period, Karl pulled down a key rebound to get his team the ball. Sam Pitts hit a short jumper with the clock running out. Summerfield won by one point, 63–62. The Rebels were state champions!

Karl had so much fun that he never skipped his studies again. When his junior year started, he began working closely with Coach Moss on developing his inside game. Coach Moss had played center in college, and he taught Karl some of his special moves. Karl had a tendency to move from side to side too much. "You have to learn to go straight up, Karl, and come down in the same spot on the floor that you lifted up from," Coach Moss would say.

Karl quickly showed that he was the best player on the Rebels. He always scored the most points and grabbed the most rebounds. Trouble was, he usually got into foul trouble. With Karl on the bench late in games, the Rebels would go to their secret weapon. Lawrence Fuller, the quickest boy Coach Moss had ever seen, would come in and save the day. "Lawrence would score eight or nine points in the last two minutes, and we'd win," Coach Moss says. "We would take the other team totally by surprise."

Midway through the year, the Rebels played in the title game of the Junction City Tournament near the Arkansas border. More than 3,000 fans filled the gym to see the Rebels take on Marion High, a school to the east that had a pure shooter named Bobby Joe Douglas, who averaged more than 54 points a game.

Karl got into foul trouble earlier than usual. With five minutes still left in the third quarter, Karl got his fourth foul. One more and he would be fouled out. Coach Moss put Karl on the bench to save him for the fourth quarter. The Rebels trailed by six points, but it was too early to use Lawrence Fuller, the secret weapon.

Coach Moss knew that with his top scorer and his secret weapon on the bench, his team could never keep up with Marion High and their pure shooter. So Moss instructed his team to go into a stall. They kept the ball away from the Marion players as best they could. Marion got the ball twice more in the period, and Bobby Joe Douglas scored both times. The Rebels trailed by ten points at the end of the third quarter. But it was better than trailing by 20!

Karl re-entered the game in the fourth quarter, and he brought the Rebels back to within five points. Then with three minutes to go, Coach Moss sent in Lawrence Fuller. With Karl and Lawrence as a one-two punch, the Rebels scored again and again. They finally took the lead by one point with just a few seconds left in the game. Bobby Joe Douglas took the final shot for Marion—and missed! The Rebels won the game, and the Junction City Tournament.

Summerfield High easily won its conference, and then sailed through the playoffs to reach the state championship game once again. Its opponent? Pineview High.

With college scouts in attendance at the championship game in Alexandria, Karl led the Rebels in scoring and rebounding. Summerfield beat Pineview for the second year in a row, this time by a 70–67 score.

Karl began receiving letters from all sorts of colleges. Some were prominent, like Louisiana State University, Arkansas, Oregon State, Washington State, and Texas, and some he had never heard of. Karl didn't know yet which college he would choose, but he sure liked the attention.

By this time, Karl's mother had married a man by the name of Ed Turner. Mr. Turner was a plumber, and he and

Shirley opened a general store in Summerfield. They called it "Turner's Grocery & Washateria." Karl was pleased that his mother had such a nice job.

Karl's senior year of high school was thrilling, yet filled with pressure. He had to keep fit and hone his basketball skills to impress college recruiters. He had to study and keep his grades up. Most important, he had to decide what college to attend.

Karl averaged 32.4 points and 18.0 rebounds a game as a senior, while leading Summerfield to an overall record of 39-9 and a third consecutive state title. Karl scored a season-high 49 points against Walker High from Magnolia, Arkansas. His best game, though, was early in the season, against Arcadia High in the final of the Homer Invitational Tournament. Arcadia featured a talented six-foot-seven-inch center—a boy the same height as Karl. It figured to be a real war inside. Karl proved he was ready for the college game by completely dominating his opponent. The Rebels won with ease as Karl scored 40 points and pulled down 37 rebounds—a school record.

The letters from colleges poured in, and recruiters began showing up at the front door. More than one hundred schools were calling on Karl. It got so hectic that Karl had to hide each day after school in Mr. Turner's house, which was up the street from his own. He memorized the cars of the coaches and recruiters that would pull up into his driveway. If it was a coach or recruiter that he wanted to talk to, he would send his brother Terry down the street to get him. Eventually, Karl narrowed his college choices to two—Arkansas and Louisiana Tech. Arkansas had a powerful program that competed each year in the prestigious NCAA Tournament. Karl liked Arkansas. Louisiana Tech was in Ruston, just forty miles down the road from Karl's house. His mother preferred Louisiana Tech.

In the state title game, Karl scored 27 points in an easy

60–46 win over Fenton High. Surrounded by a group of reporters after the game, Karl announced that he was leaning toward Arkansas as his college. The two schools continued to battle for Karl Malone. They called him and met with him practically every day. It got very bothersome for Karl. Finally, as signing day approached, Karl's principal at Summerfield made a deal with the two schools. On Tuesday, neither school would contact Karl, so that he could make up his mind. He would call the school he had chosen, and sign on Wednesday.

Karl couldn't concentrate in class all day Tuesday. He kept thinking about his difficult choice. Finally, on his way home, he made up his mind. He picked Arkansas.

Karl called Arkansas. Then he called his mother at Mr. Turner's grocery to tell her. Karl's mother, in turn, called Louisiana Tech coach Andy Russo. "Come up here and talk to Karl now!" she said.

The Louisiana Tech coaches drove from Ruston to Karl's house in Summerfield. They talked with him for a long time. Eventually, they convinced him to change his mind. They got him to sign with Louisiana Tech on the spot.

"I wanted to stay near home because, deep down, I'm a small-town guy who wants to be near friends and relatives," Karl explained later. "The bright lights of the big city are really not for me. I like it when you can walk down a street and say hello to everybody."

After Karl signed, the Louisiana Tech coaches drove back to Ruston. On the way, they passed the Arkansas coaches, who were on the road to Summerfield, thinking they were about to sign their man.

Chapter 4

During the summer before Karl left for college, he received some bad news. He would not be eligible to play basketball in his first year at Louisiana Tech. Karl had improved his grades in high school, but not soon enough. His marks as a freshman and sophomore were too poor to overcome, and he finished with an overall grade-point average of 1.97—just shy of the 2.0 average that colleges required. Karl was considered a "hardship case," which meant that he could practice with the team and attend classes, but couldn't play in any games his first year. He would officially become a freshman on the basketball team in the following year, *if* he maintained a 2.0 grade-point average at Tech.

So Karl lived on campus, went to school, and practiced with the Bulldogs. During games he had to sit in the stands behind the bench. It felt an awful lot like his freshman year in high school. Karl was mad. Mostly, he was mad at himself.

He decided to take advantage of his first year. He practiced hard and learned a great deal about the inside game. He studied hard and earned good grades. Most of all, he lifted

After sitting out a year Karl was not only allowed to play at Louisiana Tech, he was made the starting center.

weights. Karl spent a part of every day in the weight room, getting bigger and stronger. He gained twenty pounds of muscle.

By his second year in school, Karl was ready for basketball. It would be his freshman season.

The Bulldogs had been a good team the previous year, but they lacked an inside scorer. Coach Russo was eager to get Karl into the lineup. Karl had grown to six feet nine inches, and coach Russo made him the starting center.

Karl became an instant hit. He averaged 20.9 points and 10.3 rebounds a game, and led Louisiana Tech to a 19–9 record. The Bulldogs finished second in the Southland Conference. Karl became the first player in the history of the conference to be chosen Newcomer of the Year and Most Valuable Player in the same season.

Karl's sophomore year was even better. He averaged 19.8 points and 10.3 rebounds a game, despite being double-teamed most of the time, which helped open up the court for his teammates. Midway through the year, a local newspaper took a poll of the coaches in the Southland Conference, asking them which player in the conference they would choose to start a team. Every coach chose Karl Malone.

McNeese State coach Glenn Duhon said of Karl, "He's tough both inside and outside. He's definitely the franchise type of player."

Northeast Louisiana's Mike Vining said, "He controls both ends of the floor. He's big, strong, quick, and aggressive. He's everything you could hope for."

Lamar coach Pat Foster said, "He's so dominant. He's one of the top seven or eight players in the nation."

Karl propelled Louisiana Tech to a 26-7 record and a Southland Conference Tournament championship. More important, the Bulldogs qualified for the famed NCAA Tournament for the first time in the history of the school.

The net swings as Malone watches one of his incredible dunks sink to the court.

No one expected much of Louisiana Tech in the tournament. When the Bulldogs fell behind Fresno State 21–13 in the first round, not many observers were surprised. But Tech didn't give up. Karl scored 15 of his team's first 19 points to keep the Bulldogs close. Sophomore guard Wayne Smith hit a short jumper four seconds before the half to give Louisiana Tech its first lead, 27–25. Tech never let the lead go. The Bulldogs roared out in the second half to take a 40–29 lead, and Fresno State never got closer than eight points the rest of the way. Tech won it, 66–56.

Malone led all scorers with 24 points. He also yanked down a game-high 12 rebounds, blocked two shots, and had three assists and three steals.

Afterward, the Bulldogs learned that they would meet the mighty Houston Cougars in the second round. Houston was known as Phi Slamma Jamma because the players dunked so often. Their leader was seven-foot center Hakeem Olajuwon, who would go on to stardom in the NBA. "I've been waiting to play him a long time," Karl said. "Down home, that's all we hear, Houston and Hakeem. I'm just a sophomore, but I'm ready to play him, and I've finally got the opportunity."

Unfortunately for the Bulldogs, they would lose to Houston in the second round. Still it was a great year for Louisiana Tech, a year nobody expected.

The Bulldogs were no surprise in Malone's junior year. Some newspapers even predicted a top-20 finish. Karl Malone certainly did. "After we played Fresno State in the NCAA's last year, we knew we could play with anybody in the country," he said. "If we play hard, we can go all the way."

The Bulldogs were better than ever. In addition to Malone, Tech featured Wayne Smith at point guard and 6-foot-10-inch Willie Simmons as a shot-blocker. In a big game against 19th-ranked Louisville early in the season, Malone got into

Malone shows his disappointment as the Bulldogs are eliminated from the NCAA tournament, after making it to the "Sweet Sixteen."

foul trouble and finished the game with just four points. Other Bulldogs took charge, however, and led the team to a 73–64 victory. Two days later, Louisiana Tech was ranked in the top-20 for the first time in school history. Tech's record eventually improved to 16–2, and the Bulldogs were ranked as high as 12th in the nation.

Malone was still clearly the leader of the team. He shattered the backboard on mighty dunks in two different games. Nearly 1,000 shards of glass from the second board were mailed out by the school as souvenirs to members of the media. In Tech's first loss of the year, an 84–72 setback to Oklahoma, Malone came through with 22 points and 16 rebounds while his teammates played poorly by committing 26 turnovers. Karl showed his frustration late in that game with a massive slam dunk that knocked a rim out of balance. It took ten minutes to repair it.

Once again, Karl finished the season leading the team in scoring, with 16.3 points a game, and in rebounding, with 9.3 per game. The Bulldogs finished the year with a sterling 29-3 record and earned their second straight trip to the NCAA Tournament.

In the first round of the Midwest Regional, the Pittsburgh Panthers double-teamed Karl and held him to nine points. Tech proved it had plenty of other scorers, though, and the Bulldogs pounded the Panthers, 78–54. In the second round, the Bulldogs faced mighty Ohio State. The Buckeyes decided not to double-team Karl as the Panthers did, and Malone burned them with 27 points and 14 rebounds. Tech won again, 79–67. It was a dream come true as the Bulldogs advanced to the NCAA's "Sweet 16."

The Bulldogs traveled to Dallas, Texas, where they would play at the Reunion Arena. It was the biggest game in the history of the school. Millions of basketball fans across the country watched on television as Tech took on Oklahoma, the team that had handed them their first loss of the season. The game was close the whole way. Karl did his part for Tech by dominating the inside with 20 points and 16 rebounds. Even so, the Bulldogs lost in a heartbreaker, 86–84. Afterward, there was plenty of praise for Karl Malone.

Karl had been impressive in the classroom as well. His grade-point average was nearly 3.0. By the end of his junior year, he was getting the best grades on the team. Still, Karl knew his future lay in basketball. After his junior season, he declared himself eligible for the NBA draft. He was ready to join the pros.

Chapter 5

One by one, players were being chosen in the 1985 NBA draft. Some of them would turn out to be good pro players. Most would not. Karl waited for his name to be called. Other players went before him, players like Benoit Benjamin, Joe Kleine, Ed Pinckney, Keith Lee, and Kenny Green. Finally, with the thirteenth pick, the Utah Jazz made their selection—Karl Malone.

Karl didn't know much about the Jazz. He remembered rooting for them as a boy when they played in his home state as the New Orleans Jazz. In 1979, the team moved from Louisiana to Utah. Karl had never even been to Utah.

Karl signed a first-year contract for $168,000 and began practicing with the team. Jazz coach Frank Layden liked Malone's intensity, and Karl delivered immediately. In his first game as a pro, Karl scored eight points, grabbed six rebounds, and made four steals. The Jazz lost, 112–108, to the Houston Rockets, but Malone was impressive. After a second strong performance as a substitute, Karl was inserted into the starting lineup. He would play power forward. It was rare to start a rookie so soon, but Coach Layden couldn't keep Malone on the bench.

Karl started the next thirty games for the Jazz. He played so well that he was named "NBA Rookie of the Month" for December. Karl Malone was becoming well-known around the league.

The Jazz barely made the playoffs with a 42-40 record. They met the Dallas Mavericks in the first round, and Karl played like a veteran. He led the Jazz with 23 points and 13 rebounds, but the Jazz still lost, 101–93. Karl made 11 of 17 shots from the field, and held his opponent, Sam Perkins, to just 3 of 13. "Malone really surprised us," Mavericks coach Dick Motta said.

Malone stands outside the Salt Palace in Salt Lake City after signing on with the Utah Jazz. Frank Layden, the Jazz coach, looks on.

By his third pro game, Malone was named starting power forward. In December of the same season, he was named Rookie of the Month.

Karl had an even bigger game two days later, but the Jazz lost again, 113–106. Malone scored 31 points, his highest total as a pro.

Game Three was in Utah, and the Jazz had to win it or they would be eliminated. The Jazz built a 14-point lead in the first quarter, but gave it all back by halftime. The game was close the rest of the way. The score was tied 98–98, with 50 seconds left, when Malone launched a turnaround jumper from the foul line over Sam Perkins. It went in! The Jazz won, 100–98, on Karl's game-winner. "It's my biggest thrill ever," Karl said, "because we won, and it was a big win."

The Jazz lost two nights later, 117–113, to end their season. It was an exciting year for Karl, who was named to the All-Rookie team, and finished third in voting for Rookie of the Year.

Karl signed a new contract for $275,000 a year, and he came out with a bang. Maybe too much of a bang. He became the team's leading scorer, but he also got into foul trouble too often. One month into the season, Malone had already fouled out of two games. Coach Layden complained that Karl was being watched too closely by referees. "It's so obvious, it's a joke," the coach said. "It's like saying in football that a guy tackling too hard is playing too hard. I don't get it."

Karl agreed, saying, "I play hard and aggressive, but I don't go out and play dirty. If they call fouls on me, I'll just smile and keep playing. A smile will hurt 'em more than anything. Players have egos, but refs have egos, too. You can't make them look bad."

At the Los Angeles Forum in January, Karl scored a career-high 35 points against the powerful Lakers, but the Jazz still lost, 121–113. Magic Johnson led the Lakers with 26 points, and Kareem Abdul-Jabbar added 21. Four nights later, the two teams met again, this time in Utah. Karl scored 26

To remain at the peak of his game, Malone realized he needed to work on not only his shooting skills, but also on keeping his ego in check.

points, and the Jazz avenged their defeat with a 107–101 win. After the game, Lakers general manager Jerry West said, "Karl does so many darned things for a big guy. He runs the court, passes the ball, shoots it well. He's improved tremendously over last year."

A few nights later, in Portland, Karl scored a career-high 38 points against the Trail Blazers. The Jazz still lost, 121–113. Blazers coach Mike Shuler said afterward, "We played really well. We controlled them. Except Malone. He's an outstanding player."

By now, Karl was trying not to get a big ego. He told a reporter back in Louisiana, "I'm not really working on one part of my game. The one thing I am trying to work on is staying humble. It's easy to get away and forget where you came from."

The Jazz reached the playoffs again, and with a better record than the year before. In the first round they faced the Golden State Warriors—a team that had scored 150 points against them in a game earlier in the year. In Game One at Utah's Salt Palace, the Jazz stifled the high-scoring Warriors to win 99–85. Malone helped lead the way with 20 points and 10 rebounds, but he gave credit to his teammates. "Mark Eaton got all the big rebounds," Karl said, "and Rickey Green pushed the ball up the floor like I've never seen him before. I just kind of chipped in tonight."

The Jazz won Game Two as well, this time by a 103–100 score. It looked as though Utah would advance to the next round of the playoffs. No team since 1956 had won a best-of-five series after losing the first two games. The Warriors became the first. They won the next two games in Oakland, then came back to Utah to win Game Five by a score of 118–113. The Warriors led by as many as 22 points before a Jazz comeback fell short. Malone led the Jazz in scoring

By his third season, Malone was a superstar. He helped lead the Jazz to their best record ever, 47-35.

with 23 points, but it wasn't enough. Joe Barry Carroll scored 24 points, and Sleepy Floyd added 21 to lead the Warriors, who made crucial baskets throughout the game. "Did they miss a shot?" Malone asked in the locker room. "I don't think they did. I don't think they missed one all night."

Losing in the first round as a rookie was tough for Karl. Doing it again the following year was thoroughly frustrating. Karl was determined not to let it happen again.

During the summer, Karl married Kay Kinsey, a model who was "Miss Idaho." The couple bought a home in the Federal Heights section of Salt Lake City. Karl turned the basement into a gymnasium. The gym featured a weight room worth $100,000 that Karl got free from the manufacturer.

Karl became a superstar in his third season. He raised his scoring average to 27.7. He was the team's high scorer in 64 of 82 regular season games, including the first nine and last eight. Still, the Jazz struggled early on. It took a career-high 41-point performance by Malone in a 126–123 victory at Portland to even Utah's record at 22–22 at the All-Star break.

Karl made a name for himself at the All-Star Game in Chicago with 22 points and 10 rebounds. He enjoyed the limelight, but once back in Utah, he was more concerned with getting his team into the playoffs. The Jazz played a strong second half of the season, and won their last five games to finish 47–35, the best record in team history.

Utah faced Portland in the first round of the playoffs. The Jazz had played the Trail Blazers five times during the regular season—and won all five. Could this be the time Karl Malone's team finally won a playoff series? It sure didn't seem like it when the Jazz lost Game One at Portland.

Instead of sulking, Karl came out smoking in Game Two. He scored a game-high 37 points and yanked down 16 rebounds to lead Utah to a 114–105 win at Portland. The series was even at a game apiece, with the next two games to be played at the Salt Palace.

The Jazz continued their dominance of the Blazers in Game Three, winning it 113–108. One more victory would win the series.

In Game Four, Portland center Kevin Duckworth scored 21 points in the first half to give his team a two-point lead, 53–51. The Jazz edged back in front by two, 82–80, after three quarters. Karl wasn't about to let this chance slip away. He took matters into his own hands in the fourth quarter, single-handedly outscoring the Trail Blazers to give his team the victory. Malone scored 18 of his team's 29 points in the final period, while the Blazers managed just 16 points. Utah won, 111–96, to win the series. "Karl really came through in the clutch tonight," Jazz center Mark Eaton said.

The Jazz were excited to win a playoff series, but maybe they celebrated a little too long. They didn't appear ready to play the world champion Los Angeles Lakers in the Western Conference semifinals. In the first quarter of Game One at the Forum, the Jazz scored just eight points—the lowest first quarter in NBA playoff history. They wound up losing, 111–91. "We won't give up," Karl vowed. "This is going to be a tough series."

Karl was right. The Jazz shocked the Lakers in Game Two, winning 101–97. Karl led his team with 29 points for the second straight game. "It's just a great win for our guys," Coach Layden said. "They didn't fold. I'm so proud of them."

The Salt Palace was noisier than ever for Game Three. The Jazz coasted out to a 68–52 lead midway through the third quarter before the Lakers roared back. Utah failed to score on six straight possessions in the fourth quarter, which made matters worse. James Worthy's three-point play with three minutes to go cut the lead to just four points. "You knew they'd come back," Karl said after the intense game. "They're the world champions. We always knew they'd make a rally. That's why they have championship rings on their fingers."

The Jazz were having trouble scoring, so they had to win the game with defense. They held the Lakers to one point in the final three minutes to win the game, 96–89. "We can celebrate for a little while, " Malone said, "because, hey, I'm still shaking. But we've got to get ready for Sunday. If we can go back to L.A. ahead 3–1, it'd be a tremendous advantage."

It never happened that way for the Jazz. The Lakers showed why they were the dominant team of the 1980s by easily winning Game Four, 113–100. Malone scored 29 points for the fourth straight game, but he got little help. The Lakers got plenty of help. James Worthy scored 29 points, Magic Johnson had 24 points and nine assists, Byron Scott scored 20 points, and Kareem Abdul-Jabbar scored 20 points and had 11 rebounds.

The teams went back to Los Angeles with the series tied, 2–2. The Lakers won Game Five, 111–109. Utah trailed by ten points in the fourth quarter but kept battling, and suddenly took the lead by a point on Thurl Bailey's thirteen-foot jumper with twelve seconds left. The Lakers responded with a basket by Michael Cooper, then stole the ball and got a free throw from James Worthy. The Jazz had one last chance, but the clock ran out as point guard John Stockton raced frantically around the top of the key to find an opening.

It was the most discouraging loss in Karl's career. Back in Utah that night, he didn't sleep at all. The next day, he showed up for practice and told reporters that the Jazz would win Game Six. "I'm telling you right now, I guarantee we are going to win the next one," he said. "Then we'll see what happens to the Lakers in Game Seven."

Malone backed up his promise. The Jazz blew out the Lakers, 108–80, to force a final game. Karl scored 27 to lead Utah. Guard Bobby Hansen added 25, and Thurl Bailey had 20. "We got some great individual efforts from a lot players," Karl said. "We really came out ready to play."

The seventh and deciding game in Los Angeles was pure magic. Magic Johnson had 23 points, 16 assists and a team-high nine rebounds, to lead the Lakers to a 109–98 win and a series victory. "Today," Magic said, "I had to come out and play my game."

The Lakers would go on to win their second straight NBA championship.

Chapter 6

The Jazz had improved in each of Karl Malone's three years with the team. They won forty-two games his first year, forty-four his second, and forty-seven his third. But would the Jazz ever be great like the Lakers? If so, it would be with a new coach. Frank Layden decided to move up to the front office. Utah began the 1988–89 season with a new coach named Jerry Sloan.

Malone's fourth season was his best yet. He raised his scoring average again, up to 29.1 points. He led his team in scoring in nearly every game. He guided the Jazz to a team-record fifty-one wins in the regular season. He finished third in the league MVP voting. It was a fantastic year, marked by several brilliant performances.

In a mid-November game at San Antonio against the Spurs, Malone outplayed David Robinson by scoring 35 points, and grabbed a career-high 22 rebounds. A week later, in a 134–121 win over the Phoenix Suns at the Salt Palace, Malone scored a career-high 42 points, and John Stockton passed out 21 assists. "We could never stop them," Suns

In 1988 Jerry Sloan took over for Frank Layden as the head coach of the Jazz.

coach Cotton Fitzsimmons said. "Malone was a monster and Stockton was a monster."

By now, Karl was a favorite of fans around the country. He was voted to start in his second straight All-Star Game, this one at the Houston Astrodome. Karl had had a great time in Chicago the year before. He would have an even better time in Houston. Starting alongside Malone for the Western Conference would be point guard John Stockton—his Utah Jazz teammate.

With Karl's mother, Shirley, in the stands watching, the two Jazz players were too much for the Eastern Conference squad. Malone scored a game-high 28 points on 12-of-17 shooting, and grabbed nine rebounds. Stockton scored 11 points on 5-of-6 shooting, and dished out 17 assists, including an All-Star Game record nine in the first quarter. The West won 143–134 and Karl was named MVP, with Stockton finishing second in the voting.

At the awards ceremony, Malone held up his MVP trophy, pointed at Stockton, and said "I'll split this right down the middle with that little guy."

Stockton said, "That's Karl. Always taking care of his buddy Stock."

At the press conference that followed, Karl sat between his mother and his stepfather, Ed Turner. When asked how he became such a great basketball player, Karl pointed to his mother. "That's why I brought her up here to sit with me," Karl said. "When I was growing up, she worked two jobs and still found time for me. A lot of people said, 'What is she doing? He's never going to amount to anything.' Well, I guess they were wrong. I may be from the country. But for one day, I'm king of the city."

The fun stopped for Karl after the regular season. The Jazz returned to the playoffs, only to get swept in the first round by

John Stockton, Karl's teammate and friend, finished second in the voting for
All-Star Game MVP.

the Golden State Warriors. Chris Mullin led Golden State in scoring in all three games. The Warriors won twice at the Salt Palace, then finished off the Jazz in Oakland.

It was yet another playoff frustration, but Karl still did not quit. He worked harder in the off-season than ever before. He also played some, too. He bought a huge eighteen-wheeler tractor-trailer. Ever since Karl used to drive an eighteen-wheeler back in Louisiana when he was twenty, he had wanted to be a truck driver. "Basketball is my job," Karl said, "but this is my love. It's the whole thing: the machinery, the companionship with the other drivers, the smell of the diesel. I'd be lying if I said I didn't like being the most powerful thing on the road."

In the 1989–90 season, Karl raised his scoring average for the fifth straight year, this time to 31 points a game. The Jazz won more games than ever before, finishing with a 55–27 record. Once again, though, the team was upset in the first round of the playoffs. This time, the Phoenix Suns shocked the Jazz. Kevin Johnson hit a 12-foot jumper at the buzzer, in the fifth and deciding game at the Salt Palace, to beat the Jazz, 104–102. Karl Malone sat hunched over at his locker. "It's an empty feeling," he said without looking up.

Coach Sloan tried to give his star player credit. "Without Karl Malone, I doubt we'd even make the playoffs," the coach said. It was a nice thing to say, but it didn't make Karl feel any better.

It was an upsetting year for Malone in another way, too. Despite having his best season, he wasn't voted to start the All-Star Game. He would get to play as a substitute, but it was a blow to his ego. "This is a slap in the face," Malone said. "I'm nobody's sub." Karl was determined to prove himself. He came out in his next game and scored a record 61 points. It was the most points scored in the NBA in three years, since

Karl Malone puts one up over the hand of the San Antonio Spurs' David Robinson.

Michael Jordan did it in 1987. The Jazz beat the Milwaukee Bucks, 144–96, and Bucks coach Del Harris said, "I knew he'd come out and make a statement, but I didn't think he'd write a whole book in one night."

By the 1990–91 season Malone was widely recognized as the best power forward in the game. Clyde Drexler of the Trail Blazers said that Malone was so good "he should be outlawed."

All the recognition in the world couldn't change another typical year for the Jazz. Utah acquired sharp-shooting guard Jeff Malone to take some of the scoring pressure off Karl. Still, Karl led the team in scoring average again with 29 points, and also in rebounds with 11.8. The Jazz had another great regular season record at 54-28. Once again in the playoffs, the Jazz were frustrated, this time in the second round by Portland. The Jazz lost one game by two points, another by three, and the deciding fifth game by seven. Karl led the Jazz in scoring and rebounding in all five games. Again, he did what he could. Again, it wasn't enough.

The Jazz played at a new arena for the 1991–92 season—the Delta Center. It seated more than 19,000 compared to the Salt Palace, which held fewer than 13,000. That was the only change concerning the team. The Jazz cruised through the 1991–92 season in typical fashion, led by Karl's 28 point scoring average. Utah tied a team record for wins with 55. Would another playoff failure follow?

Karl's temper and sportsmanship were questioned during the season after a hard foul on Detroit's Isiah Thomas. In the first quarter of a game at the Delta Center, Thomas drove toward the hoop. Malone came off his man to defend. Both players went up in the air. When Thomas landed, his face was a bloody mess. Malone's right elbow had opened a gash which required forty stitches to close. Malone was charged

Phoenix Suns forward Tom Chambers battles with Malone. The Suns upset the Jazz in the first round of the 1989 NBA playoffs.

with a flagrant foul and was fined $10,000 by the NBA. Several Detroit players accused Malone of playing dirty. Other observers said there was nothing intentional about the play. Either way, Karl felt terrible about the incident. He called Isiah at his hotel to clear the air. He told Isiah the foul wasn't deliberate. They remained friends.

As the Jazz prepared for the playoffs, they read a comment in the newspapers made by San Antonio Spurs forward Terry Cummings. It said, "Utah has been known to crumble at the end." This angered the Jazz, partly because they knew it was true.

Karl saw plenty of reasons why Utah could win in the playoffs this time. "It's the first time we have guys who are athletic and who want to play. I have a better feeling now than the year we took the Lakers to seven games."

Sure enough, the Jazz were a better playoff team. First, they got past Danny Manning and the Los Angeles Clippers in five games. Karl led the Jazz each time in scoring and rebounding.

Next, they rolled over the Seattle SuperSonics, 4 games to 1. Karl had 37 points and 13 rebounds in the clinching game, a 111–100 triumph at the Delta Center.

Suddenly, for the first time ever, the Jazz were one series from the NBA championship games. They had to play Portland, the team that tripped them up in the first round the year before. It would be no different this time. The Trail Blazers won the first two games at Portland. The Jazz came back to win the next two at the Delta Center. Game Five at Portland was the big one. If the Jazz could somehow win, they could clinch the series at home in Game Six. They almost did. Down by eight points at the half, the Jazz fought back without point guard John Stockton, who was poked in the eye in the second quarter and never returned. Utah miraculously tied the

Many doubted that the Jazz could get beyond the first round of the playoffs, but Malone knew his team was ready.

game on a three-point shot by backup point guard Delaney Rudd with five seconds left. Overtime! The Jazz jumped out in front, but the Blazers reeled off eight straight points to win, 127–121.

The Utah players returned home deflated. It showed in Game Six as Portland won, 105–97. Still, it was the best playoff performance the Jazz and their fans had ever experienced.

Right after the season, Karl experienced something else wonderful. He got to play on the USA Olympic Team in Barcelona. He was among a dozen NBA superstars who comprised "The Dream Team." Jazz teammate John Stockton was also on the team as it coasted through the Olympics undefeated to win the gold medal for the United States. "It's a dream," Karl said. "Ten or fifteen years from now down the line, I can look back and have the gold medal, and tell my kid, 'Hey, I played on the team.' "

The 1992–93 season began optimistically. It got even better midway through the year when the All-Star Game was played at the Delta Center and Karl Malone and John Stockton led the Western Conference to a 135–132 overtime victory. Karl scored a team-high 28 points, grabbed 10 rebounds, and blocked two shots. Stockton scored only 9 points, but he handed out 15 assists, grabbed 6 rebounds, and made 2 steals. The Utah fans were given a special surprise when it was announced afterward the Malone and Stockton were named co-MVPs. "Being able to win it with Karl makes it even more special for me," Stockton said.

Karl averaged 27 points a game to lead the Jazz to a 47-35 record and yet another playoff appearance. It marked the seventh straight year that the Jazz reached the playoffs since Karl had joined the team. The Jazz, unfortunately, were

Malone goes up to put one over the Denver Nuggets center, Dikembe Mutombo. Despite many setbacks, Karl Malone continues to fight for a championship.

eliminated in the first round by the Seattle SuperSonics in five tough games.

Karl and the Jazz reached the playoffs again in 1994. He plays for $3 million a year now. He continues to lift weights and get stronger. "The paint is where men are made. That's where I earn my living," he says. "Nobody ever takes me one-on-one. When one guy can stop me, that's when I retire."

Malone is disappointed that he hasn't won an NBA championship. He has accomplished everything else in basketball, though. He certainly has enjoyed his career so far with the Jazz. "The best thing that could've happened to Karl Malone," he says, "is coming to Salt Lake City. I'd love to win a championship, but, honestly, not so much for myself. You can believe this or not, but I'd love to win it for the true fans who have watched me grow."

Career Statistics

COLLEGE

Year	Team	GP	FG%	REB	PTS	AVG
1982-83	Louisiana Tech	28	.582	289	586	20.9
1983-84	Louisiana Tech	32	.576	282	601	18.8
1984-85	Louisiana Tech	32	.541	288	529	16.5
Totals		92	.566	859	1,716	18.7

NBA

Year	Team	GP	FG%	REB	AST	STL	BLK	PTS	AVG
1985-86	Utah	81	.496	718	236	105	44	1,203	14.9
1986-87	Utah	82	.512	855	158	104	60	1,779	21.7
1987-88	Utah	82	.520	986	199	117	50	2,268	27.7
1988-89	Utah	80	.519	853	219	144	70	2,326	29.1
1989-90	Utah	82	.562	911	226	121	50	2,540	31.0
1990-91	Utah	82	.527	967	270	89	79	2,382	29.0
1991-92	Utah	81	.526	909	241	108	51	2,272	28.0
1992-93	Utah	82	.552	919	308	124	85	2,217	27.0
1993-94	Utah	82	.497	940	328	125	126	2,063	25.2
Totals		734	.525	8,058	2,185	1,037	615	19,050	26.0

Where to Write Karl Malone

Mr. Karl Malone
c/o Utah Jazz
Delta Center
301 West South Temple
Salt Lake City, UT 84101

Index